The brain has some pretty amazing stuff in it. I'm going to tell you about two parts that affect me. The first is the Prefrontal Cortex. It's located in the frontal lobe here.

Prefrontal Cortex

The Prefrontal cortex is responsible for most of our very-human traits, as it is the most evolved part of our brain.

Including:

- Logic & complex thinking
- Planning & decision making
- Attention
- Judgment
- Time perception
- Impulse control
- Social behavior

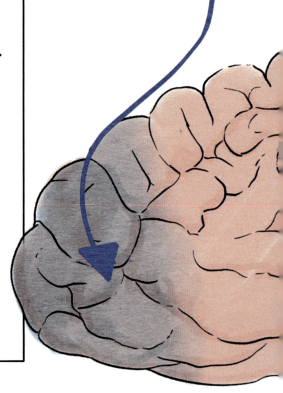

> The second part of the brain I'd like to tell you about is the Amygdala. It's an itty bitty tiny thing way down deep inside the brain.

Amygdala

> The Amygdala, in contrast, is the prehistoric "reptilian brain" where many of our survival instincts reside. It is rigid and compulsive.
>
> Including:
> - Fear conditioning
> - Emotional learning
> - Memory
> - Behavior
> - Libido

> Let's talk a bit more about the Amygdala, as our relationship is a bit more, well, "complicated..."

Now remember that itty bitty Amygdala? Well, instead of turning "on" when needed, mine is ALWAYS on.

That means my brain is constantly signaling that there is danger, Danger, DANGER! Adrenaline is in my body all the time.

They call this "chronic irritability" in the brain field. It means that I am always on alert, ready to fly into action at the slightest sign of danger!

While you might not run into many bears in your home town, there are many other things that can stimulate this "Fight or Flight" response in every day life.

- Being put on the spot

Facing a fear -

- A near miss

For most people, this is a good thing. It keeps them safe. It turns on when needed, so you can divert from danger.

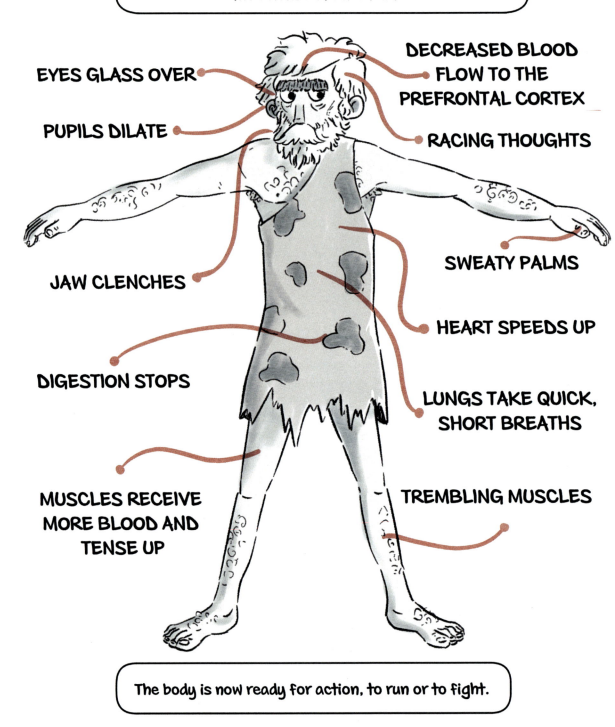

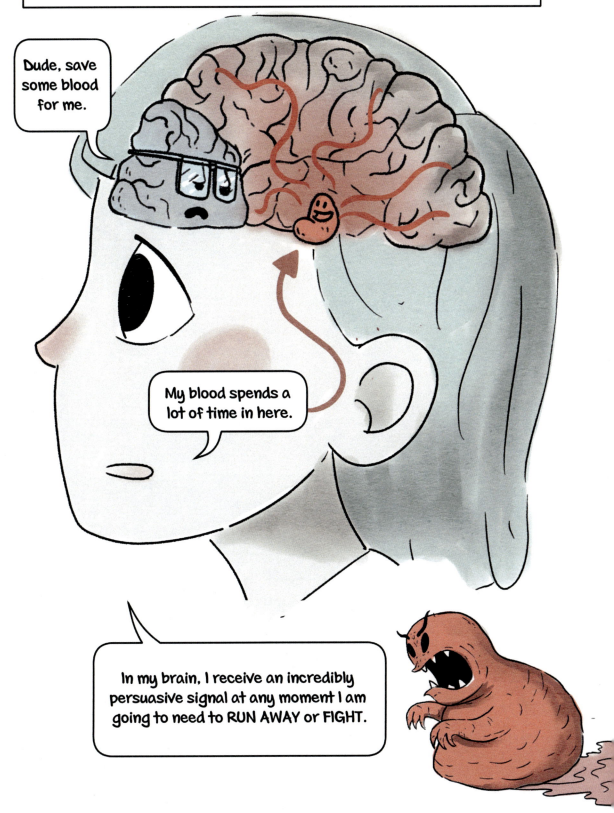

In fact, studies have shown that the stress caused by frustration can cause a drop in up to 30 IQ points. This means that the ability to make a calm, rational decision is pretty much impossible.

In the ADHD brain, (a common dual diagnosis) the Prefrontal Cortex is often delayed in maturity and growth by up to 3 years. This means that a kid with ADHD is about 2-3 years immature, and may sometimes behave like a younger child. (Like I didn't have enough issues!)

Read on to learn how I react when my "Fight or Flight" response is triggered...

Instead of running, my brain might decide to fight instead. This can mean arguing, yelling, or even hitting if I feel threatened.

I don't like it when I Fight. It's even worse when I Rage.

These "Temper Tantrums" or "Rages" have been likened to an Emotional Seizure. No one can stop a seizure. It has to run its course, and all you can do is protect the seizing person from harm.

RAGE 101

HOW TO HELP

- DO NOT ENGAGE – if able, allow outburst to run its course safely

- Calm demeanor, palms out, non-threatening

- Express empathy. Ask, "Can I do anything to help?"

- Don't Reason

HOW TO HELP

- Give space, but keep me within eyesight

- Don't approach or attempt to move me

- Don't Touch Me

- Only if self or others are in danger do you attempt a hold

If I am treated gently and appropriately, I might snap out of it. If I am touched or provoked, a Rage can last up to an hour. I need help recognizing when I can turn things around, because remember, my brain is 2-3 years behind

SENSORY DYSFUNCTION

Remember I mentioned the senses being near the Amygdala too? Ding ding ding!

This means my sensory needs can be wonky, and that I'm extra sensitive to, well... EVERYTHING!

Music

Loud NOISES

Brussels sprouts

Slow cars

Fast cars

Textures

Clocks and clicks

Cold

SILENCE

Smells

Heat GRASSHOPPERS

Wind gust

Background NOISE

You'd think this guy would be exhausted, with all that hyperactivity!

HOW TO HELP

- Be aware of triggers
- When stressed, sensory problems increase
- Be aware of increased irritability, which increases sensory sensitivity
- Pay attention to cues that senses are overloaded
- Encourage good diet & frequent snacking (protein)

SOCIAL PERCEPTION

Sometimes my social perception can be off because of my ADHD and hyper Amygdala tendencies. I might think others are out to get me when they are not. It makes games rather difficult. Even if someone is offering to help, if I'm extra irritable, I might see them as threatening.

Sorry Poppy, we have a full team.

You can't play because we hate you.

It's a bummer to always expect the worst.

Tag, you're it!

I tagged you because you're bad at this.

It's Sarah's turn to go first.

Sarah is going first because Ms. S. likes her more than me.

HOW TO HELP
- Reframe situation "How would you feel if..."
- Use relevant, personal examples
- Explain rules prior to games
- Coach & role play being "out"
- Talk, talk, talk

"I need lots of help to be my best self, because I'm a kid who's still growing and learning. Here's some things you can do to help me succeed."

- Positive reinforcements (like, all the time)
- Warnings before transitions
- Reminder of rules prior to ALL games
- Use routines and post a clear schedule of the day
- Frequent, daily reminders before PE and recess of behavior expectations
- Leadership roles! (I love to feel helpful.)
- Reassurance after I make mistakes
- Fierce hugs and encouragement
- Empathy and forgiveness

"And most importantly, I need Understanding. I need Empathy. I need you to know that I am struggling with an invisible disability, and that my behavior does not always reflect who I am. I need guidance, reassurance, and love while I learn to manage this guy →"

Bibliography

Dillon, K. (2018) Sensory Anxiety: Not your ordinary anxiety. STAR Institute for Sensory Processing Disorder. Retrieved June 14, https://www.spdstar.org/node/1129

Dingman, M. (2014, June 24). Know your brain: Amygdala. Neuroscientifically Challenged. Retrieved June 14, 2019, from https://www.neuroscientificallychallenged.com/blog/know-your-brain-amygdala

Greene, R. (2014). The Explosive Child: A new approach for understanding and parenting easily frustrated, chronically inflexible children. New York, HarperCollins Publishers.

Harvard Health Publishing. (2018, May 1). Understanding the Stress Response. Retrieved June 14, 2019 from https://www.health.harvard.edu/staying-healthy/understanding-the-stress-response

Neurobehavioral Systems. (2019). Neuropsychiatry. Retrieved July 1, 2019, from https://neurobehavioralsystems.net/for-parents/what-is-neuropsychiatry/

We would also like to say a special thank you to all of our friends and family who have supported us on this journey. We could not have done this without your support, knowledge, empathy, and love while we made this book. Thank you to Kelli Draves, Kat Olson, Brittany Bagwell, Amy Wardlaw, Kiezha Ferrell, Dr. Ghazal Ghaysar, the team at UCLA Semel Institute for Neuroscience and Human Behavior, and all the fellow parents who struggle daily to guide these challenging kids.

Made in the USA
Columbia, SC
01 February 2022